MERCHANTS:

A Sunday Evening Lecture,

BY T. W. HIGGINSON.

" A certain prelate once exhibited to the holy saint Thomas Aquinas, great vessels precious coins, saying "Behold! Master Thomas, now can the church no longer say, St Peter said, Silver and gold have I none!" "True," replies the saint, "neither n she say what immediately follows: In the name of Jesus Christ, rise up and walk."
[Heraud's Savonarola.

NEWBURYPORT:
A. A. CALL, PUBLISHER,
HUSE AND BRAGDON, PRINTERS.
1851.

This lecture was one of a course now in process of delivery, by the author, in Washington Hall, Newburyport, on alternate Sunday Evenings; and it is now published by request.

January 29, 1851.

LECTURE.

Upon Merchants, their duties, dangers and opportunities, there is much to be said; much more than can well be introduced without devoting a special evening to the systematic consideration of the matter, and I have, therefore, announced it as the subject of my lecture to-night. And though I have never been a Merchant, technically speaking, myself, yet I think that fact should not interfere with your hearing what I wish to say.

For, first, there is the ordinary opportunity given to me of knowing, through observation and sympathy, the position of others.

Secondly, I do not ask you to believe anything I say because I say it, but only to take it for what its intrinsic truthfulness makes it worth.

And thirdly, there is a sense in which in this community all are Merchants, since all must use money, in a greater or less quantity, as all must breathe air; commerce is bargaining, and the smallest bargain engages one, so far, in commercial life. You buy or sell the smallest thing—a stove, a book, or a penknife—and in that purchase or sale you have the experience of a merchant; the interest you take in the progress and result of your bargain, its honesty or dishonesty, its economy or extravagance—all give to you the very identical hopes and fears, and pains, and pleasures, and perplexities of the merchant; and when one grows to be a millionaire, and buys or sells ships or towns, or empires, I am persuaded that it is only the same thing over again.

One of the most eminent literary men of this country once told me that many years since, when a boy on a farm, he had permission given him to sell for himself a calf of his own raising; and that he remembered so vividly the struggles of mind he then went through, the bitter anxieties of hope and fear, the intense temptation to extort more than the animal was strictly worth, and to contrive little plots to conceal its defects and exaggerate its merits, that the experience came back to his mind to this day, when he felt especially indignant at the basenesses of commerce, and made him more charitable to the offender, remembering that he also had been tempted.

Perhaps there is a lurking corner in all our consciences in which this story does not appear quite unintelligible; and assuming it to be so, I shall go on to speak of Merchants and Commerce as freely, though not, perhaps, as amply and accurately, as if I were one of the fraternity myself.

It is always claimed, and must be conceded, that Merchants stand well in history; since the history of civilization is to a great extent the history of commerce. The narrative of the discovery of new lands, of the establishment of friendly intercourse between different lands and of free institutions in those lands, is to a great extent the narrative of the progress of commerce.

When Cæsar resolved to visit Britain, he says that the interior of that country was altogether unknown, excepting to Merchants. Commerce in the fifteenth century sent Columbus to the West and Vasco de Gama to the East, discovered two new worlds, and revolutionized the trade and politics of the old one.

"If we trace commerce (says Hume) in its progress through Tyre, Athens, Syracuse, Carthage, Venice, Florence, Genoa, Antwerp, Holland, England, [and America] we shall always find its seat in free governments." The feudal system of the middle ages was destroyed by the rise of free cities, and commerce created these, and all our modern civilization dates from them.

So commerce has fostered mildness and the arts of peace. It was a constant complaint among ancient nations that it caused the love of war to decay. "Among the wandering tribes of Arabia the seeds of knowledge and refinement (says Gibbon) go where the caravans go, and *the Merchant is the friend of mankind.*" The great religious wars of the Middle Ages were merged in commerce; much of the trade of modern Europe dates from their close. "The beautiful coins and the beautiful stuffs of Asia had done much to reconcile our merchants with the Mohammedan world. The merchants of Languedoc were ever passing over into Asia, cross on shoulder, but it was to visit the market of Acre rather than the sepulchre at Jerusalem; and so far had religious antipathies given way to mercantile considerations, that the bishops of Maguellone and Montpellier coined Saracen money, had their profit on the minting, and discounted the impress of the crescent without scruple. Richard Cœur de Lion wore at Cyprus a silk mantle embroidered with silver crescents."*

So commerce has usually opposed itself to all disturb-

*Michelet's France. Am. Ed., I. 256.

ance of existing peace between nations. The commercial spirit of England resisted the rupture between this country and the Motherland. Merchants in the British House of Commons defended the liberties of America. And it is stated in the most recent and able history of England, that "the English Merchants offered to pay the taxes on the colonies, or a substitute for them, rather than risk losing their trade."*

Now there is something certainly impressive in this coincidence of interest and duty which has thus made a great mode of human activity, at the same time a great channel of God's providence; commerce is certainly ennobled by it. For these are historical facts; and it is plain that things must be thus; for obviously, one would say, there can be no trade where there is not some degree of intelligence, and habits of comfort and refinement; there can be no trade where there is either constant war between nations, or jealousy and non-intercourse between nations—the common alternative in the ancient world; there can be no trade where there is entire monopoly on the part of a few, and the many can neither buy or sell freely; and so it is plainly true that the merchant *is* the friend of mankind, and that even his selfishness serves God.

Thus far is the common argument. But does it, after all, go quite far enough? Is it ever the case that selfishness does the highest work of God, and can it ever be relied upon for unmixed good? I doubt it, and I think we must look with a closer eye at commerce. True, up to a certain point, it is plausible, this plea of mercantile influence; up to this present stage of civilization it has

* Pictorial History of England; quoted in a valuable article on "The Influence of Commerce," in Hunt's Merchant's Magazine for Dec., 1850, to which I am otherwise indebted.

freed nations and helped society forward, but is it always to be trusted? There is the anxiety. Up to a certain point it is good, it sets man free by setting itself free; but its basis is admitted to be selfishness; the merchant does not go out of his way and give up anything to civilization, he civilizes men on speculation; and there is no such great merit in that. "Mirabeau," said the French satirist, "is capable of doing anything for money, even a good action;" but the remark was never considered a compliment. Can we say no more for the Merchant, and is this ground enough for trusting him. Suppose an exigency to arise in which interest looks the other way; nay, suppose a whole stage of civilization reached when his interests are all secured, trade is free, and any farther change, though it may help others, must hurt him! He has freed men from other tyrannies; now will he free them from his own? He has traded in human rights; will he refuse to trade in human wrongs? He purchased civilization; will he refuse a profitable investment in barbarism?

I am suspicious as to the answer; for there is a test case ready made to our hands.

The African Slave Trade; a traffic now so condemned by the civilized world, and even by republican slave-owners, that for years no word has been uttered in its defence—how long has it been so condemned, and against whom was that victory won? *Against the spirit of commerce;* the fact is beyond denial. Every plank of that bloody deck was defended, inch by inch, by merchants.—Up to a certain point that great power had sustained freedom; beyond a certain point it stood as firm against it. Let its interests once cease to be identical with those of humanity, and humanity must yield. Consider the facts. When the immortal Wilberforce exposed to public gaze the secrets of that horrid traffic, his biographer says, "The first burst of generous indignation promised nothing less than the instant abolition of the trade, but *mercantile* jealousy had taken the alarm, and the defenders of the West India system found themselves strengthened by the independent alliance of *commercial* men." *

Again, opposition to Wilberforce's motion "arose amongst the Guinea *merchants*."

The Corporation of Liverpool spent, first and last, upwards of £10,000 in defence of a traffic which even the gravity and calmness of judicial decisions have since pronounced "infernal."

"Besides printing works in defence of the slave trade, and remunerating their authors; paying the expenses of delegates to attend in London and watch Mr. Wilberforce's proceedings; they pensioned the widows of Morris and Green, and voted plate to Mr. Penny, for their exertions in this cause."

It is said that the Corporation of Liverpool, at this time, "believed firmly that the very existence of the city depended on the continuance of this traffic."

The Aldermen of London also testified that "if the trade were abolished, it would render the city of London one scene of bankruptcy and ruin!" They were willing, however, to put the trade under "*wholesome regulations*," as in that case "it would be productive of *greater commercial advantages!*"

The newspapers of the time were filled with predictions "that the revenue of the country would be half annihilated by this measure. Its naval strength would decay. Merchants, manufacturers and others, would come to beggary." And the members from Liverpool summed

* Life of Wilberforce, as quoted in Mr. Mann's letter to his constituents.

up the character of the measure as "unnecessary, visionary, and altogether impracticable." *

Even so late as 1816, the same class of men in the same country opposed the abolition of white slavery in Algiers, from the same base motives of interest. It was thought that the danger of navigating the Mediterranean, caused by the Barbary Corsairs, was advantageous to British commerce, because it might deter the merchant ships of other countries from visiting it. †

These things we need remember when we hear (as I have often heard from sincere and intelligent merchants) the claim made that because commerce has always been the friend of liberty, therefore it always will be. Especially at the present time, when an issue is raised between right and wrong, where it is openly attempted to throw the influence of commerce all on one side and bear down everything by its weight—do we need this remembrance. The commerce of Boston and New York says not one word against the anti-slavery agitation which was not said by the commerce of Liverpool against that of the subject of the slave trade; only that the terrors which are now raised when a schooner is built in South Carolina, or stock taken for a cotton factory in Georgia, had then a more immediate stimulus and a surer foundation.

Let us now speak of the general position of the merchant in our society.

* See Clarkson's Hist. Abol. Slave-Trade, for these and many facts as striking. Mr. Alderman Watson asserted that the West India trade depended upon the African, and the Newfoundland fisheries upon that; "the latter could not go on, but for the vast quantity of inferior fish bought up for the negroes in the West Indies, and quite unfit for any other market." Mr. Grosvenor candidly admitted that the Slave-Trade was "certainly not an *amiable* trade; neither was that of a butcher, yet both were necessary. It was not an amiable trade, but he would not gratify his humanity at the expense of his country's interests; and he thought we should not *too curiously inquire into the unpleasant circumstances connected with it*;" which strongly reminds us of many speeches on slavery, and especially that of the northern member who refused to inquire into the horrors of Washington slave markets, on the ground that "he had no taste for such things."

† This seems scarcely credible, but see the facts in Sumner's Lecture on this subject.

The day is long past when commerce was considered in its very essence and theory fraudulent; and the day is past *here* when it was regarded as an ignoble calling. Yet the wisest man of ancient Rome once wrote that "they who buy goods that they may sell them again are base and despicable men, since they can only make a profit by practising some deception." And again, when pronouncing all retail traffic wholly contemptible, he seems to think it a great admission to allow that commerce on a large scale may not be altogether base.* "A law prevailed in Thebes, (says Aristotle in his Politics) which forbade any tradesman from holding a public office unless he had shut up shop for more than ten years."

And in the monarchical countries of Europe at this time, even in England, I suppose that no merchant, as such, (that is, none unless deriving rank from some other source) could be admitted into the highest social circles.

Now all these abstract objections to commerce, as an employment, whether the prejudice be a moral one or a conventional one, seem manifestly unjust. In the *theory* of commerce I can see nothing in the least objectionable. Even the popular objection, more current among us than any of these—that the merchant *produces nothing*—seems to me unfair. For when society is organized, and each man no longer creates and prepares his own food and clothing, and labor is lightened by being distributed—then the products of labor must be distributed also, and that is a new labor. The merchant is not a producer, but he is a distributer of products, which may be equally laborious, or more so, and is certainly as legitimate an occupation. Goods must be carried from place to place—tea

* "Sordidi etiam putandi, qui mercantur quod statim vendantur. Nihil enim proficiunt, nisi admodum mentiantur. * * * Mercatura autem, si tenuis est, sordida putanda est; sin magna, copiosa, non est admodum vituperanda." Cicero de Offic. I.

from China, cotton from New Orleans, gold dust from California—and there must be somebody to attend to this transportation and delivery; and as it must be done systematically, accounts must be kept—and so every merchant, be it on the largest or smallest scale, is in fact either a porter or a book-keeper, or both.

So there always must be merchants in every state of society beyond the very simplest. But it may easily happen that as commerce may be out of its true position in one state of society, and underrated—so it may be out of its place in another state of society, and overrated; this may happen in several ways, and several evils flow from it. I think such is the case now.

I. There is this danger, that at particular times and places trade may become too attractive, may be thought easy compared to other employments, more honorable, and offering a greater *chance*, even if not a certainty, of splendid successes. The sober mechanic, tired of steady work, day in and day out, with little excitement or promise of any splendid profits, hears with envy the tale of mercantile speculations, fancies them far more brilliant than they are, and longs to take his share. He plunges in and adds one more to the competitors, of whom there are so many already that they shudder at the thought of a new one, and so it goes on. Dr. Channing estimated that the number of persons actually engaged in commerce, large and small, was more than twice the number actually needed to carry on exchanges; and on this point, as on others, I have often heard his practical sagacity admitted. In view of the facts, I do not see how it can be doubted. It would seem to show little knowledge of the economy of organization of labor to doubt that if, for instance, all the dry good stores and grocery stores of this town were concentrated into two or three of each, with proper buildings and arrangements, at least *one-half* the present amount of attendance could be saved, and the public as well or better served. (I do not say that this could be done without other changes in society, but I think that if it were, these would be the consequences.) Now since the mercantile class produces nothing, and only exists to facilitate communication, it is evident that for every merchant too many there is a producer too few, and the balance of society is lost; hence excess of competition, failures, "ruinous sacrifices"—or else frauds on the purchaser, adulterations, even destruction of property*—or illegal and immoral expedients, as smuggling, false invoices, false bounties on fish, and the liquor trade, without which I am constantly told that no grocer or victualler in this town can make a living.

II. This is the beginning of evil. Then arises the danger that the mercantile class, becoming thus unnaturally large, and concentrated in towns where they hold not only the balance of power but an overbalancing power, will be led to overrate their own importance—so to overvalue it that they forget the simplest facts of political economy. I remember to have seen this statement in the Boston Daily Advertiser some time since, "*Commerce being the source of wealth*," &c., &c. Commerce the source of wealth? As well say that canals are the sources of the rivers which they connect. Yet one can easily believe the writer really to have thought so. For as the great English Engineer, Brindley, on being examined before the House of Commons, and asked what he seriously supposed to be the object for which rivers were created, replied that it was to feed navigable canals; so anything upon which we fix our attention sufficiently becomes the

---

* As in the well known case of the Dutch spice trade.

centre of the universe to us, and the sun, moon and stars, only revolve around it.

I remember another passage in the same newspaper, at the same time. In speaking of some attacks upon Mr Winthrop, it terms them "slurs upon the Merchants of Boston and *their representative.*" Now the population of Boston is 138,000; and I find in the Boston Almanac of this year, the whole number rated as merchants, including commission merchants, to be about 600; and supposing this number to be only one-tenth of the whole number, counting the retail trade, clerks, &c, we shall have 6000; or supposing it to be one-twentieth, 12,000; who could hardly, one would think, claim quite to monopolize the representative of a population of 138,000.

How much of the history of legislation in this country, has been the history of this same exclusive commercial spirit, which here shows itself. It has for years been one of the great contending forces in every political battle, and, though dislodged successively from every position, on Bank, Sub-treasury and Tariff, has every time died hard. Nay, it has shaped political precedents to suit itself, and the present Secretary of State regards the "main object of the framers of the constitution to have been [not, as stated in the preamble, to ordain and establish liberty, but] to aid and protect trade and commerce!"

The largest item of national expenditure for the current year, (that of the Navy Department*) is incurred confessedly for the protection of commerce; while its annual expenses were estimated a few years since by an experienced merchant of a neighboring town as fully equal to the *whole annual profits* of our foreign trade; in other words

*Naval appropriations for the current year $8,935,552; war ditto [including fortifications] $8,481,138; Civil and Diplomatic ditto $7,648,306.

a payment for insurance of 100 per. cent on the value insured; an investment which would be hardly tolerated were merchants themselves called upon to pay the premium.§

The same predominating influence is seen in such maxims as that laid down by Mr Webster, in his New York speech, as the basis of his Union party: "The one great object of government *is the protection of property.*" Now the strength of the merchant lies in his property, real and personal; deprive him of it he is weak, he only knows how to buy and sell what he needs; not to make it. But the strength of the mechanic is in his mind and his hands, he may lose all his property, and still be rich enough to be independent as ever. A young man fails in business; if no property is left we call him unfortunate, what can he do without a cent in his pocket? But how many an Irish laborer, how many a fugitive slave comes among us without a cent in his pocket—nay, with scarce a whole pocket to hold a cent—and give him but a chance to use his hands, places himself above want. Tell him of your theory of government—"that it exists to protect property"—what property has he to be protected, what property have the majority of any community except strong hands which protect themselves?

And how is it with the question acknowledged on all sides to be *the* great political question of the present day? "Slavery," says a distinguished foreign observer, "besides being a political question, and the shuttlecock with which politicians are playing their game of conciliation, to win power and place, is a commercial and trading question also. The chain that commences in New Orleans or

§See the celebrated tract of Mr S. E. Coues, of Portsmouth, N. H. entitled "What is the use of the American Navy," for elaborate calculations, which have never been answered.

Texas, extends itself in unbroken continuity along the seaboard to Portland. The interests of the slave-holder, and the interests of the merchant, the agent, and the manufacturer, are intimately blended. These classes sympathize with each other. The chord that is struck at Galveston vibrates to Boston. The classes at the North, thus identified with the system, are the wealthy, the active, the influential, and the powerful, in their own several localities. They are the leading politicians—they patronize and support the press—they can command the co-operation of those who are dependent upon them—and they have the means, by public meetings, resolutions, and the control of the daily journals, of making loud and imposing demonstrations. They have done this often before, when they thought their interests were in danger. They did so in the days of John Randolph, who, upon the floor of Congress, once said:

"If this great agricultural nation is to be governed by Boston and New York, and Philadelphia, and Baltimore, and Norfolk, and Charleston, let gentlemen come out and say so, and let a committee of public safety be appointed from these towns, to carry on the government. I am forcibly struck," he continued, "by the recollection of a remark made (in the English House of Commons) by Sir Robert Walpole, who said that 'the English country gentlemen (poor meek souls) came up here every year to be sheared; that they laid mute and patient, whilst their fleeces were taking off; but if he touched a single bristle of the commercial interest, the whole sty was in an uproar.'"

III. I pass to the *personal* dangers of commercial life.

1. There is the danger of too great absorption in the details of trade. Doubtless a man must be willing to labor for his bread; but as it is unhealthy to the body to think too

much of our bread as we eat it, so it is bad for the soul to think too much of it as we earn it. Disguise it as we may, there is something in the divine spirit of man so utterly foreign from day books and ledgers, that it refuses to be all concentrated on them, and the attempt to enforce such concentration ends in spiritual suicide. It is safe and right to trade in order to live, but if we live only in order to trade, we die. After all there is a certain point beyond which the human virtue of prudence ceases to be a virtue, and becomes penuriousness. There is a certain noble generosity and indifference in the use of money which commerce does not love and "success" may not follow, but whicn nature loves and God loves. The world judges a man by what he has received, but God and nature ask also what has been given. A man gains house, lands, fame, wealth, station, power, and the world calls him successful in his life's bargain. But suppose he has sold his virtue, sold *himself* to obtain these things, and then where is the gain and the success? Suppose his heart, and his manliness, and his great thoughts and principles are all gone to pay for these things, then what are the possible returns that can make *that* bargain a successful one? I do not say that the world is not a good judge according to its own standard. I do not say for instance that a man who sells first his time, and then his freedom, and then his soul, for a million dollars, does not make a better bargain than he who sells his time, and his freedom, and his soul, for fifty; but I do say that either of them makes a bargain to which the honest bankrupt is a millionaire—and that the poorest outcast who lies lonely, sick and starving, in some bleak hut by the hill side, with every wind of heaven sweeping through upon his bed of straw, may lead a noble and a beautiful life in comparison with either

I know this is not the current prejudice of our time and place. "The first thing to teach a boy," said once an honest and sincere minded father to me in the presence of his son of six years old—"the first thing to teach a boy *is the value of a dollar*—that's what I call the corner stone." The satire is not mine but his. He was a gentle and kind-hearted man, but that was his theory, at least on week days, at his place of business; nor did it occur to him that he had said anything which Adam in Eden might not have remarked to Eve. Practically it is the philosophy of many or most. I think it is essentially the philosophy of Benjamin Franklin, whom we should have long since canonized, if we canonized any body in these parts. A recent English writer, after placing Franklin at the head of those who believe in "living by bread alone," sketches the whole American people as standing behind one long counter, from Maine to Texas, trading against the rest of the world, under the auspices of this guardian saint.* "A penny saved is a penny got," Thomson calls a "scoundrel maxim."

I know that this is only one side, one half the truth, but there is no danger of its over-balancing the other half. If I were to talk of it a whole day and night it would do you no harm, for will not the world's voices talk for the six coming days and nights on the other side far louder? As in that adjoining street there stand two great buildings side by side, the factory and the church, and day by day from Monday to Saturday the clatter and roar of the factory fills the street, and then for one day the vast machine pauses and lets the voice of the preacher echo faintly through closed doors upon the passers by, and then begins again Monday morning, as busily as ever, for another six day's

*Leigh Hunt's Autobiography.

roar and clatter;—so through all our society is the spirit of business as six to one to anything else, and there is no fear of stating the higher wants of the soul so strongly as to more than counterbalance it.

2. I pass to another personal danger of commerce; its tendency to accustom the soul to a lower standard of virtue than the christian standard of absolute universal love. Is it not true that the prevalence of competition through almost all branches of traffic, in all but the smallest towns, is such as to make it almost accepted as a fixed axiom that "you cannot carry the golden rule into trade ?"

I do not venture to assert that this statement is without exceptions. I willingly believe in the possibility of occasions where the dealer may think of others as well as himself; if he makes little or no profit on a bargain, *may* enjoy the thought that the purchaser has a better bargain out of it; if he loses a chance of profit himself, *may* willingly hear that his neighbor up street has gained it. And if there were enough business (or believed to be enough) for all—as it may be, for instance, in small villages where there are but one or two stores—I dare say this would frequently be the case. But how is it commonly ? *A man must live,* he thinks; there is not business for all; his neighbor's gain is his loss; it is care enough for him to look out for number one, without troubling himself to look out for his neighbor also. "Besides," he says, "my cussomer, or my competitor, is a sharp man, more so perhaps than I am,—I wish to have the bargain fair, certainly; but if I look to his interest, he will nevertheless look to his interest, and there will be *two to look to his interest* and nobody to look to mine. Whereas, it is now an understood thing, a contest of wits, like two lawyers arguing, it being agreed that each shall do the best he can for one side, and that this plan works best on the whole." Very well, very well, but observe that in all this you do not deny that which I asserted, but only try to excuse it—namely, that you do *not* carry the golden rule into trade. You explain how it is that it is arranged so, but you do not prove that this habit of looking to your own interest and leaving your neighbor to look to his, however well it worked in practice, did not prove in the end to warp and wither mind and conscience, as the one-sidedness of lawyers has always been admitted to do!

Let us take an actual case where all the circumstances were as favorable as will ordinarily happen, and see how it looks when the highest test is applied to it.

"A. and B. were two merchants in Liverpool. A. was willing to sell 500 chests of tea from his warehouse, and B. was willing to buy them, but objected to the price. So A. went home out of town, thinking no more of the bargain. B. lived near him, but staid in town an hour longer. Meanwhile the news comes in of a rupture with China and a rise of a pound a chest in the price of tea. B. therefore calls on A. on his way home, and says, "I have decided to give you your price for those 500 chests." A. acquiesces and B. goes home, having cleared £500 ($2500) by that hour's work."*

Now here there was no falsehood told, no direct dishonesty practised. The price asked was paid, and perhaps a profit was made on it. It was not B.'s fault if A. did not know as much as he did about China; "perhaps he did; it was not his business to ask." But suppose he had reasoned differently; suppose he had had a sudden twinge of brotherly love and had said to A.,—"Why should I have all the benefit of this accidental advantage. Tea has risen £1 a chest and you shall share my profit, have 25 per cent. of it

*"Remedies for the Perils of the Nation. Page 81.

at least! I ask you—would not one shout of laughter have gone through the Liverpool Exchange when the story was told? Now I will not inquire whether *you* would have laughed or not, my friends; but I put it to you, in the midst of that bargaining and that laughter, *what became of the golden rule?*

Or take another case. Two merchants on the same wharf in Boston, hear at the same time of a fall in the price of coffee at Rio Janeiro, and decide to despatch ships to take in a cargo there. One has a ship already, will freight her for that port and can do it in a few days; the other cannot charter and equip one for a fortnight, perhaps longer. "My rival will have a fortnight's start of me," he says, despondingly, "I must give it up," but he looks at the vane; "No! the wind is wrong—his ship cannot leave the harbor—let me make haste and I may outwit him yet." He hastens, he labors, he works all day and dreams all night of his project; day after day the wind remains contrary: day by day he exults in his neighbor's misfortune, which is to be his gain—(legitimate gain, no foul play, observe;) his last prayer at night, his first in the morning—if he dares to say to God what he says to himself—is *that his neighbor may still be thwarted in his plans, and the contrary wind still hold;*—week after week finds him absorbed in this one thought of defeating another's hopes;—but stop! my friend, what, in the midst of this fortnight of anxiety, has become of that little *Golden Rule?*

Observe, I am not a merchant, I do not say how all this can be helped; if you say to me, that my objections are all theory, and if I undertook to enter trade myself I could do no better—then I can only say, you are admitting my proposition, which you might sometimes deny, that *one cannot carry the golden rule into trade!*

I have lately had the privilege of reading the early correspondence of a noble man, who, though bred to trade, soon quitted it in disgust, and became Minister-at-large in Cincinnati, in which office he was spared long enough to show himself one of the wisest practical philanthropists whom this country has produced. The crisis of his dissatisfaction with commerce seems to have arrived when he first went to the West Indies on a trading voyage. "Be thankful," he writes to a friend on the day after his arrival, "that you are not a merchant. See how I am placed.—A gentleman invites me to his house, treats me as kindly as possible, does all in his power for me, and what then? Why, I must—*must*, observe—try to bargain him, coax him, drive him, cheat him, out of a dollar or two. I'd rather lose a leg; and yet if I don't I'm a fool, a greenhorn, and he'll take me in, because I would not serve him. If ever I get home, I'll quit trade for ever."*

Dare you smile at that impulse of noble disinterestedness, oh, young man? Look well to your soul, for the base alloy is tarnishing it already. You are one for whom it is not safe to have had your life fall in these trading days. Go back a little to times of fresher impulses, times which you boast that your commerce has uprooted, and learn that chivalry has a lesson to teach you yet. Study such a life as that of stout Godfrey of Bouillon, conqueror in the first crusade, of whom it was rejoicingly written "that if all the honor of all men on the face of the earth was totally corrupted and destroyed, the honor left in the soul of Duke Godfrey would alone be enough to revive and restore it all;" and tell me if, should the hero come back to earth to-morrow, you would venture to invite him

---

*Memoir and Writings of James H. Perkins; I. 47.

down and station him for one little half hour behind your counter in Newburyport?

I have lately, however, been reading an Essay* which quite ably defends the spirit of Commerce as an essentially Christian spirit, upon this plausible theory, *that commerce demands the prosperity of both the trading parties.* "Merchants must cease to sell when their customers grow poor. They consult their own interest by consulting that of others."

Stated more pointedly, this sentiment seems to be this: do not shear the sheep too close. As kind old Isaac Walton says of fishing, "when you put the worm on the hook, handle him as if you loved him." Make as good a bargain as you can out of your customer, but stop short of making him a pauper, for then, instead of trading with him, you will be taxed for him.

This plausible argument ends very nearly where that argument for slavery ends, that it is for the master's interest to feed and clothe the slave, and keep him in good condition, that he may get more work out of him. But unhappily these conditons are not hard to fill, and experience has shown that you may keep a slave in excellent working order and yet make his way of life far less decent and far less comfortable than that of the cattle and horses which are sold from the same auction block; and so in trade, a dealer may keep his customers in excellent trading order, and yet keep them on the verge of starvation or bankruptcy. And as on some plantations, sugar plantations for instance, it is found cheaper to consume slaves year by year and buy new ones to replenish the stock, than to remit the work and keep the same set of victims—so

* In Hunt's Merchant's Magazine, to which I am also indebted for some preceding remarks.

we see the same terrible exceptions in our community, and your financiers, from the rich Boston broker down to the underground rum-seller of country back streets, will grind down a hundred customers not into powder but into paupers to-day, and make their fortunes out of a hundred new ones who flock in to be ground down to-morrow.

Talk to these men about "caring for the interests of their customers." Secure in the possession of an ever-renewing harvest of victims, they laugh you to scorn.—Their circle is large enough to last their three score years and ten. They will not need, like Alexander, to cry for another world, after they have made this one bankrupt. "Is not this ample room?" they ask; "when Newburyport is exhausted, there is Boston; when Boston is exhausted there is fair game in New-York; exhaust New-York, and there is still London, and Paris, and Vienna, and Russian loans, and all the business machinery of all the Rothschilds. "Truly they say to us innocents—in the words of a noted European statesman—"you are unskilled in the art of fishing in so vast an ocean as the pockets of an hundred million people!"

I think we had best let these men go and not attempt to convince them that honesty is the best policy. Reverse the motto, and they will like it better—for policy is their only honesty.

3. And this brings me to the third and last danger of mercantile life—its danger to common honesty. Setting aside the *golden rule* of loving one's neighbor as one's self; and what we may call the *silver rule* of setting one's affections on things above, not below; how is it with the simple *copper rule* of "Honesty is the best policy." Does that hold in commerce?

I must confess that the persons who excite my suspicions most against merchants are the merchants themselves, when I see the excitement produced among them when any *one* does an honest act—for instance, pays his debts after failure. It is remembered for years, and whenever the name of the individual is referred to, it is trumpeted to his honor. Now, although it is pleasing to see this theoretical respect for simple honesty, still, when we look closer, it is alarming that it should be so rare as to be talked about. Thus I remember reading in Anson's voyages that nearly all the shops in Canton have on the signs the words "Pau Hou," or "no cheating here." Now when a man thinks it necessary to announce on his sign "no cheating here," though it does not demonstrate that he does not cheat, it proves pretty conclusively that some of his neighbors do; and the more general the announcement, the greater the suspicion; and so of this similar phenomenon in our mercantile community. If it is so generally understood that honesty is the best policy, pray why this sensation when any one is politic enough to try it?

I sometimes think that the habits of caution prevalent among us, the excess of documentary transactions, notes, endorsements, receipts, have rather a tendency to encourage fraud, by constantly suggesting the thought of it, and seeming to reduce the whole thing to a game of skill. I have been confirmed in this by hearing that in places where there is less attention to these things, and more trust in honor, the trust is better repaid. For instance, I am told that it is so in the West Indies and Spanish America generally. Mr. Schoolcraft, who was Indian agent at Lake Superior for twenty-five years, said that he had never known an Indian to break a promise in the way of business. I read in a recent essay on the commerce of

Brazil* that the slave-trade being contraband is carried on entirely upon honor, "and hence," the author adds, very simply, "fraud is of rare occurrence." One wishes trade in general could be declared contraband, if such be the result. And there is an anecdote in point of Mr. Fox, the British statesman. A tradesman who had often dunned him in vain for payment of a note, came in one day and found him with two hundred pounds before him, and claimed his share No, said Mr. Fox, this is for a debt of honor I owe to Sheridan. Then, said the tradesman, I make my debt a debt of honor, and threw the note in the fire. Mr Fox acknowledged the obligation and paid him at once.

But to return to our own affairs. My friends, or those of you who are merchants I am not afraid to ask the question, Is honesty practically found the best policy? Does it make men rich most rapidly? Let me suppose a case and tell me if it is an ideal case.

A young man goes to church and hears a sermon preached from this maxim. It is illustrated. Two characters are sketched, one a simple and truthful youth—the other a knave—but always a very transparent knave, not one of the deep kind. Their career is described; the knave comes uppermost at first—the virtuous youth afterwards, (it is easy to have it so;) knavery ends in the Penitentiary—virtue in wealth, honors, joy for this life and the next. The doctrine is very satisfactory; temporal comforts and eternal at one stroke; and our young man goes out to try the experiment.

He is placed in a store. His master possesses capital, energy, coolness, some talent and *some* honesty,—i. e. he would like as well to be honest as not, if nothing were lost by it. Our young man has a sensitive conscience, far more sensitive, he soon finds, than his master's. False pretences,

*North American Review, April 1849.

evasions, even direct falsehood occasionally; he is soon shocked. "This man" he says, "is not what I supposed him; nor what others suppose him, certainly—for he has a fair reputation." But soon a new puzzle. He has reason to suspect that those who deal with his master understand him, yet they are not shocked, but perhaps bow and cringe if his master is richer than they. How is this? He consults his father, and his friends, and confides with some hesitation his suspicions. How are they received ?

One well meaning but ignorant father might reply. "Matters cannot be as you think, my son—your master is one of our leading men, director of the Bank, member of the church, a most respectable person. You must be altogether mistaken. Beware of hasty judgments, my son!"

Another father, more sagacious, but not prepared to take any responsibility in the matter, might simply shrug his shoulders and seem to say "this is a matter I cannot interfere with. You had better let it rest."

And a third, very likely would say to his son, "do not be so ready to judge your betters, young man. I want you to be a practical man, not a foolish visionary; try to imitate your master, and if you can become as much of a man as he is, I shall be satisfied and so may you be."

Then comes the trial for the young man's soul. If it is a sensitive and noble one,it may receive a permanent shock; but more generally the careless easy youth takes the matter much as his father has done and says to himself that if he wants to "succeed" he must do as others do—and that he *must* "succeed" has been always laid down as the corner-stone of life. Thus it goes on, our young merchant gradually becoming more and more a practical denier of the preached doctrine of "honesty the best policy" and should he sometime go back to church and hear the old sermon preached over again, how will it strike him? Sitting in the full consciousness that he is daily gaining money and power and honor by petty departures from honesty, if not larger ones, how can he help saying "this is all abstraction, not practical sense; it does for the young and simple, not for me; and if this is a specimen of what they call religion, it is all equally an assumption!" And so he goes away, his heart hardened forever.*

My friends, I agree with him so far as this—that for one I do not believe that honesty is the best policy, so far as this world's external gains and honors are in question. And I think if it were so, and honesty were pursued as policy, it would cease to be honesty and become a mere manœuvre, not wrong perhaps but no way meretorious. Doubtless the highest success is to be found in doing right, but it is not what men of the world call success, and it is not to be got by seeking it selfishly. It is truly written that he who would save his life shall lose it, and only he who is willing to lose it for Christ's sake, shall find it. It seems to be ordained that the interest of one is the interest of all, but it seems to be also ordained that this is not plain to any one, until he has ceased to think of his own interest. If you try to make others happy you yourself become happy, but not if you do it *in order* to be happy, for then you are thinking of yourself and not of them. "God gave the world these directions," says the Persian Touriat, "Oh world, be servant to him who is servant to me, not to him who is servant to you."

Righteous, in its Saxon derivation, means right-wise; and the fear of the Lord is truly the beginning of wisdom. When some one told old Bishop Latimer that the cut-

---

*Compare "The Tradesman's Sermon," an Essay by a friend of the author, in "The Present," (No. 4, New York, 1843) to which I am much indebted.

ler had cheated him, making him pay two pence for a knife not worth a penny. "No," said Latimer, "he cheated not me but his own conscience." Alas, how often it happens thus around us every day; life is taken up in obtaining, by hook or crook, the means to support life; "to make a living" is the only object of labor—and what is the end of it;—only the body lives after all—and all the higher faculties of the soul, love, honor, integrity, courage—these sink, decay and only *make a dying*.

Young men, who hear me, and who are committed to a commercial life, will you not think of these things? Some of your temptations and opportunities you know better than I, because I am only a looker on—others I know better than you, for the same reason. If what I have said of the dangers of a mercantile life is not a fair statement of what it must be, but only a warning of what it may be—then prove it by taking the warning. Prove by your life that a merchant can live nobly in his profession—can be a merchant and still live a life of truth, of love, and of heaven. There is nothing intrinsically wrong in wishing for pecuniary success, and it is often a good feeling at bottom which stimulates it. All young men wish to obtain an influence, to gain a standing in the community; all their hopes of usefulness rest on that. Therefore they wish to stand well at every point; to come up to all the current standards, to have nobody look down on them on any ground. Even a wise man may feel something of this. If one went to teach a savage nation, who had no standard of merit but skill with the bow and arrow, one would naturally like to be found a good marksman; first equal or excel them on their own ground, and then lead them a step farther. So a young man in this community, wishing to do as others do, belongs to a military company, or an Odd Fellows Lodge, or is a vote distributor every November, or gets chosen to General Court, if possible—but above all, *makes money*; and then he has earned his freedom, stands on his own foundation, and no one need look down on him. He has gained "an independence" literally.

So far so good ; but the danger !—the danger is that the end is forgotten in the means, and by the time he has got money, he has forgotten how to use it ; he wants general enlightenment, thought, reading, observation, knowledge of society, practical beneficence, faith in any new idea. Poor creature ! he has staid underground in his gold mine till his eyes are as blind as the sightless fishes of the Mammoth Cave ; and so finding that he cannot escape out of money-making into anything else, he goes back to that again, and burrows a little more.

"But surely (you say) this disastrous change will never come to me. I will not be one of those old men yonder who have spun their souls into gold, and point to that as the only result of their life's career." But do you not know that every one of those old men said the same thing when he was young ? Few men are born as base as the exclusive love of money-making renders many. Guard against the temptations which have made them what they are.—Remember those stern strong words of old Scripture, "As a nail sticketh fast between the stones of a wall, so doth sin stick close between buying and selling." Buy and sell with your inner eyes open, as well as your outer—lest while you protect yourself from being cheated by your neighbor, you cheat yourself out of something more precious than anything he can ever get from you. Among the ancients it is said that Plutus, protector of merchants, was also God of lies, and he still teaches his followers to deceive themselves quite as often as they deceive each other.

It is well to be independent; but it is a sham independence which is bought with money. It is well to show what good can be done with wealth; but it is better to show what good can be done without it. Whence have come the great examples of this world thus far, from the rich or from the poor? Ponder the answer of St. Thomas Aquinas to the prelate who once exhibited to him great vessels of precious coins, and said, "Behold, Master Thomas, now can the church no longer say, as St. Peter said, Silver and gold have I none!" "It is true," replied the holy man "neither can she say what immediately follows, 'In the name of Jesus Christ, rise up and walk!'"

But lastly, as there is nothing noble in commerce on the most magnificent scale, save for its uses; so there is nothing ignoble in trading on the smallest scale, save for its abuses. "It is honorable" says Horace Mann, "either to handle a yard-stick or to measure tape, unless it makes the faculties of your soul no longer than the one and no wider than the other." Live in your occupation so as to ennoble it while you stay in it; when the nobleness ceases, let the occupation cease. Your opportunities are great—every act of trade gives you a chance to show the difference between a true upright man and a base manœuvrer. If you do not find it so, do not stay in it, no, not on any conceivable pretext; no not even that last one of all that you "must get a living." It is the old plea of sin. 'Tis what the French thief said to the priest long since. "But it is necessary that I should live, sir—and I have no other way." "I do not see that necessity, friend," was the calm answer. Friends, it is *not* necessary that you and I should live, for has not many a man died before now rather than live basely? It is not necessary that we should live—still less that we should gain the happiness and honors of life; but it is necessary, it should be felt as necessary by each one of us, that we should not soil our white raiment with one spot of baseness. *First the kingdom of God and his righteousness*, oh young man, dare to write this for the motto of your ledger, and then you may dare to be a Merchant.

www.ingramcontent.com/pod-product-compliance
Lightning Source LLC
LaVergne TN
LVHW020742120826
845150LV00010B/2356

* 9 7 8 1 4 1 8 1 9 4 3 7 6 *